How Do You Know It's Winter?

by Ruth Owen

Consultants:

Suzy Gazlay, MA
Recipient, Presidential Award for Excellence in Science Teaching

Kimberly Brenneman, PhD
National Institute for Early Education Research
Rutgers University, New Brunswick, New Jersey

BEARPORT
PUBLISHING

NEW YORK, NEW YORK

Credits

Cover, © Tony Campbell/Shutterstock, and, © Eric Isselée/Shutterstock, and, © Harper/Shutterstock, and, © Steven Russell Smith Photos, and, © Neirfy/Shutterstock; 4TL, © Blend Images/Superstock; 4BL, © Steve Byland/Shutterstock; 5, © Pics-xl/Shutterstock; 6L, © Losevsky Pavel/Shutterstock; 7, © Songquan Deng/Shutterstock; 8L, © Caleb Foster/Shutterstock; 8B, © Blend Images/Shutterstock; 9, © Igumnova Irina/Shutterstock; 9TR, © Evgeny Tomeev/Shutterstock; 10, © joingate/Shutterstock; II, © Cattallina/Shutterstock; IIR, © Gary K. Smith/FLPA; 12TL, © FotoYakov/Shutterstock; 12BL, © FotoYakov/Shutterstock; 12R, © Jurgen & Christine Sohns/FLPA; 13, © Jaroslaw Grudzinski/Shutterstock; 14L, © IgorKa/Shutterstock; 14R, © Vasilius/Shutterstock; 15, © leonid_tit/Shutterstuck; 16L, © Glenda M. Powers/Shutterstock; 16R, © Lindsay Dean/Shutterstock; 17, © Photo Researchers/FLPA; 18L, © Al Mueller/Shutterstock; 18R, © James Horning/Shutterstock; 19, © Chris Alcock/Shutterstock; 20L, © Vishnevskiy Vasily/Shutterstock; 20B, © Ann Cantelow/Shutterstock; 2ITR, © Rossario/Shutterstock; 2IC, © oliveromg/Shutterstock; 22TL, © Madlen/Shutterstock; 22BL, © EtiAmmos/Shutterstock; 22RC, © Melica/Shutterstock; 22R, © Le Do/Shutterstock; 23TL, © LlaneM/Shutterstock; 23TR, © Peter Baxter/Shutterstock; 23BL, © Vishnevskiy Vasily/Shutterstock; 23BC, © joingate/Shutterstock; 23BR, © Elena Elisseeva/Shutterstock.

Publisher: Kenn Goin
Senior Editor: Lisa Wiseman
Creative Director: Spencer Brinker
Design: Emma Randall
Editor: Mark J. Sachner
Photo Researcher: Ruby Tuesday Books Ltd.

Library of Congress Cataloging-in-Publication Data

Owen, Ruth, 1967–
  How do you know it's winter? / by Ruth Owen.
     p. cm. — (Signs of the season)
  Includes bibliographical references and index.
  ISBN-13: 978-1-61772-397-1 (library binding)
  ISBN-10: 1-61772-397-5 (library binding)
  1. Winter—Juvenile literature. I. Title.
  QB637.8.O94 2012
  508.2—dc23
                          2011044939

For more information, write to Bearport Publishing Company, Inc., 45 West 21st Street, Suite 3B, New York, New York 10010. Printed in the United States of America in North Mankato, Minnesota.

10 9 8 7 6 5 4 3 2 1

Contents

Winter Is Here

Every year is made up of four seasons—spring, summer, fall, and winter.

As fall comes to an end, winter arrives.

The air outside may feel cold.

Animals may have to dig under the snow for food.

People may avoid the chilly weather by staying indoors and drinking hot chocolate.

Each year, winter starts on either December 21 or December 22. The first day of winter is marked on calendars.

December

Su	M	T	W	Th	F	Sa
						1
2	3	4	5	6	7	8
9	10	11	12	13	14	15
16	17	18	19	20	(21)	22
23	24	25	26	27	28	29
30	31					

first day of winter

4

What is the weather like in winter where you live?

The Shortest Day

playing outside in the dark after school

As winter nears, each day brings more hours of darkness than light.

It may even be dark when kids get out of school in the afternoon.

The first day of winter is the shortest day of the year.

This means there are fewer hours of daylight than on any other day.

In winter, on the same day each week, draw a clock that shows what time it got dark. How much later does the sun set each week?

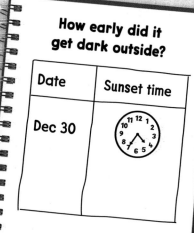

How early did it get dark outside?

Date	Sunset time
Dec 30	

Once winter arrives and the shortest day has passed, the number of hours of daylight each day starts to increase again.

Snowflakes and Gloves

Longer hours of darkness and shorter hours of daylight are not the only clues that it's winter.

The weather is colder in winter than at other times of the year.

In many places it snows.

When it's too cold to go outside without a coat, a hat, and gloves, winter is here!

a snowy day

warm winter clothes

Place a thermometer outside. Check the temperature at the same time every morning for a week. Write it down. Does the temperature change or stay the same?

Weather Chart

Date	Temperature
Monday	40°F (4°C)
Tuesday	32°F (0°C)

Sometimes winter weather brings huge blizzards! A blizzard is a very big snowstorm with lots of wind.

a blizzard

9

A Winter Rest for Plants

When you can't see flowers or green leaves outside, it's a clue that winter is here.

In winter, it is too cold for most plants to grow.

Their leaves and flowers die, but their **roots** stay alive underground.

When the weather warms up in spring, the plants will grow again.

potted plants in winter

In winter, go outside and look at the trees around you. How are they different from the way they looked in summer or fall?

shoots

bulb

roots

Below the ground, flower **bulbs** wait for spring. When the weather warms up, they will send **shoots** above the ground. Soon flowers will bloom.

Bare Branches

By winter, many trees have lost all their leaves, and their branches are bare.

The trees look as if they have died.

They are still alive, though!

The trees are just resting until they can begin growing again in spring.

a tree in fall

a tree in winter

Raccoons often make their homes inside trees. A hole inside a tree is a good place to stay warm in winter!

raccoon

bare branches

Some trees have bare branches in winter. What do you notice about other trees?

Staying Green

Some trees stay green all winter!

They are called evergreen trees.

These trees have tiny green needles on their branches.

needles

evergreen tree

Unlike trees that lose all their leaves in fall, an evergreen tree doesn't drop all its needles at the same time. It drops some needles and grows new ones all year round. That's why it's always green.

See You in Spring!

When the weather cools down in fall, some animals go to sleep for the whole winter.

A groundhog spends winter asleep in its cozy underground home.

A grizzly bear digs itself a place to sleep called a **den**.

These animals do not wake up until spring!

groundhog

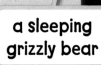

a sleeping grizzly bear

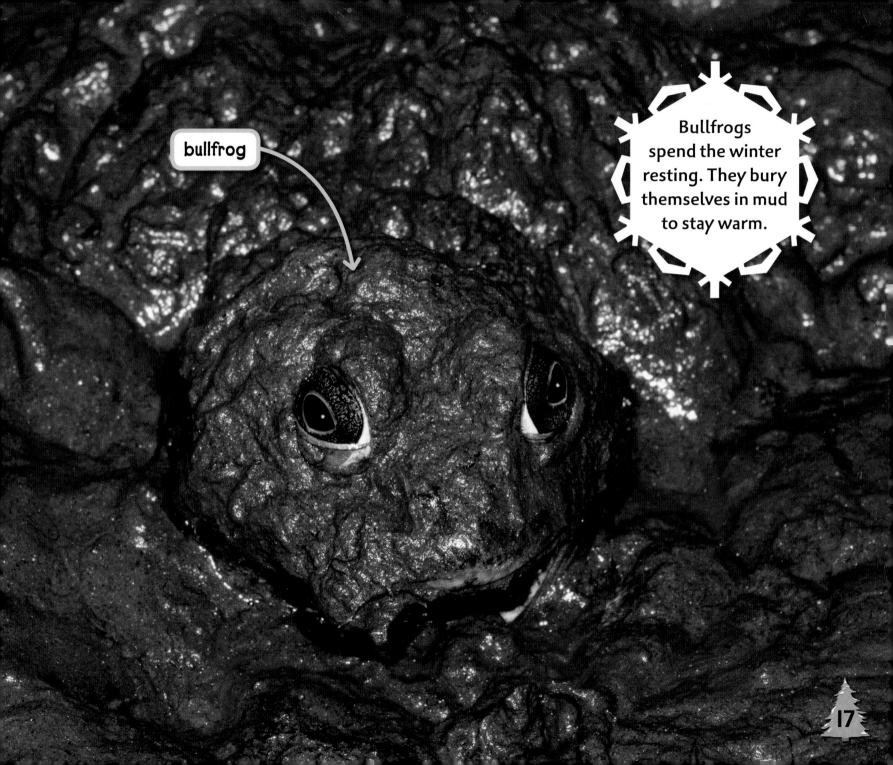

bullfrog

Bullfrogs spend the winter resting. They bury themselves in mud to stay warm.

17

Hungry Birds

In winter, there is not much food around for birds.

It's not easy to find the seeds or insects that they eat during the rest of the year.

Many people help birds by hanging up bird feeders outside their homes.

The birds visit the feeders to fill up on seeds and nuts.

bird feeder

Sometimes hungry squirrels visit bird feeders to eat the nuts and seeds!

squirrel

In winter, watch a bird feeder for ten minutes, and count the number of birds that visit.

bird feeder

Winter in a Garden

In winter, snow sometimes covers the ground.

People have to shovel the snow off their driveways.

Kids play in the snow and make snowmen.

Icicles often hang from the branches of trees.

Gardens are hidden under a blanket of snow.

Winter is the season when plants rest—until spring arrives.

icicle

See if you can spot animal footprints in the snow or mud. What kinds of animals do you think made them? Can you figure out where the animals were going or where they came from?

raccoon footprint

Winter lasts until March 20 or 21. Then spring arrives.

21

Science Lab

When you are in your backyard, on the playground at school, or in the park, go on a winter treasure hunt.

See how many of the things on the Winter Treasure Hunt list you can see, smell, hear, touch, or collect.

If it's not winter where you live, then draw a picture of winter.

Include as many things from the list as you can.

Then when winter comes to where you live, go outside and try to find the things you put in your drawing.

Winter Treasure Hunt

Things to see

A tree with bare branches

A tree with needles

A bird's footprints in snow

A bird eating at a bird feeder

Some berries

Something frozen in ice

A snowman

Things to smell

A cold morning

An evergreen tree

Things to hear

The wind howling

Snow falling from a tree branch

Things to touch

The bark of an evergreen tree

Soft, new snow

Things to collect

A pine cone

An icicle

A twig from an evergreen tree

Science Words

bulbs (BUHLBZ) the rounded underground parts of some plants; food for the plant is stored in the bulb

den (DEN) a home where wild animals can rest, hide from enemies, and have babies

icicles (EYE-si-kuhlz) long, thin spikes of ice that form from dripping water on wintry days

roots (ROOTS) long, thin underground parts of plants that take food and water from the soil

shoots (SHOOTS) the parts of new plants that first appear above the ground

Index

Read More

Cassino, Mark, with Jon Nelson, PhD. *The Story of Snow: The Science of Winter's Wonder*. San Francisco: Chronicle Books (2009).

Enslow, Brian. *Winter Colors (All About Colors of the Seasons)*. Berkeley Heights, NJ: Enslow Publishers Inc. (2012).

Glaser, Linda. *It's Winter! (Celebrate the Seasons)*. Brookfield, CT: Millbrook Press (2002).

Learn More Online

To learn more about winter, visit

www.bearportpublishing.com/SignsoftheSeasons

About the Author

Ruth Owen has been developing, editing, and writing children's books for more than ten years. She particularly enjoys working on books about animals and the natural world. Ruth lives in Cornwall, England, just minutes from the ocean. She loves gardening and caring for her family of llamas.